Tales from the Edge of the Woods

TALES

from the Edge

of the Woods

by Willem Lange

University Press of New England

HANOVER AND LONDON

*To Erik, who went ahead to show the way;
and Ida, who stayed behind to help*

University Press of New England, Hanover, NH 03755

Printed in the United States of America

5   4   3

CIP data appear at the end of the book

The pieces in this book first appeared in the
Valley News, Lebanon, New Hampshire.

Contents

Not Love at First Sight   1

The Old Canoe   5

Favor Johnson   10

The White-Footed Mouse   18

New England Reeling   22

The Child of Fear   26

Gals at the Bor'as   32

The Old Man's Legacy   37

Baddy and the Fawn   42

All Gone Away   46

Kids on the Sideboard   50

Sliding on a Shovel   54

Blood Brothers   58

Dear Olivia   61

The Carpenter and the Honeybee   65

Pop? It's Honey   70

The Old Man at Solstice   75

Well Grounded in Mechanics   79

Tales from the Edge of the Woods

Not Love at First Sight

I first saw New England many years ago, in September of 1950. I cannot say that it was love at first sight.

I came here, you might say, as the wages of sin. I'd been living happily in Syracuse, New York. Too happily, as it turned out. The juvenile authorities of Onondaga County finally decreed that, one way or another, I was going away to school that fall.

My father was a traveling missionary, and was often away doing the Lord's work. My mother, who was deaf, diffident, and alone, couldn't handle me, and I was starting to get into some serious trouble. The social worker down at the courthouse said that I needed some male authority figures. So my parents found a boys' prep school where tuition was low, the ambiance was religious, and where the students performed daily manual labor as part of the curriculum.

The school was in Massachusetts, in the Connecticut River Valley, which I understood to be in New England. I knew nothing at all about New England, except that the people there came from Old England, wore black jackets and knickers with big pewter buckles on their pants and shoes, and walked through the snow each Thanksgiving with their families and guns to celebrate the holiday.

They were very stern and moral and religious. They were also very proud to have ancestors who'd come over on the Mayflower.

Thus on a September morning my father and I drove down the Mohawk Valley, crossed the Hudson River at Albany, and followed the twisting Mohawk Trail over the Taconic Mountains. In mid-afternoon we descended into the Connecticut Valley, drove through the gates of the school, and found the Admissions Office. About an hour later, I watched the taillights of my father's Chevy disappear down the road.

As a late applicant, I was assigned a room in the attic of a faculty home. Here I met my first Yankee, the man of that house. He will remain forever in my memory the quintessential Yankee schoolmaster: tall, rawboned, laconic, and brown, dressed always in brown shirt and tie and dull brown three-piece suit. He'd graduated from Bowdoin and the University of New Hampshire. He taught mathematics. He suffered from dyspepsia—either that, or he was not happy to see me. He was also very strong. I watched him bring my cot up from the cellar, holding the iron frame horizontally by one end and raising it before him as he came up the attic stairs. I guessed that he was probably a male authority figure. In any case, I never gave him any trouble.

Breakfast the next morning was at seven fifteen in the dining hall. I closed the door of the house behind me a little before seven and stepped into another world.

Thick fog lay over everything. The path before me disappeared a few yards away. As I followed it, hidden bushes and fence posts loomed up on either side. Where the sky was open, it shimmered yellow toward the invisible sun.

There were still elm trees in those days. They reared up above me, great, threatening creatures with arms spread and hanging down. I touched their rough, wet bark for assurance as I went by. Then there was the chain-link fence of a tennis court, followed by the dark, indistinct bulk of a dormitory. I began to hear voices in the mist, and soon I joined a stream of students headed for breakfast.

The day before me seemed ominous. But I know now that fog on a September morning in New England portends a beautiful day. I walked to my eight o'clock Latin class across a campus still shrouded in golden mist. By eight thirty the classroom windows were all open to the sun.

My schedule called for two hours of sports after lunch, followed by two hours of work. So about three thirty I showed up for work, with a dozen or so of my fellows, at the Farm Office at the lower end of the campus.

The boss there divided us into crews to dig potatoes, clean the piggery, report to the cow barns, and pick apples. I got apples.

And I met the second Yankee of my life, Mr. Taber. He was tall and bulky like the first one, but much older and stoop-shouldered, wearing bib overalls, gold-rimmed spectacles, and the first blue denim frock coat I'd ever seen. He moved and talked slowly, and had the fascinating habit of repeating the last few words of almost every sentence he spoke . . . he spoke. We could tell he was pretty leery of this green crew come to destroy his beloved orchard, but we were all he had. Each of us got a wooden ladder and a bucket that hung over one shoulder and had a cloth bottom that could be released to let out the apples.

It was a cool afternoon, my first one ever in New England. The bright apples, small and hard as billiard balls, flowed from the tree into my bucket and then gently into the waiting boxes on the ground below. Two hours seemed to pass very slowly. As the sun dropped toward the hill beyond the playing fields, cold air flowed down into the orchard. I remember the chill at my collar, the ache of the strap over my shoulder as the bucket filled, the rung of the ladder under my foot. The smell of apples, sweet and tart in the fading afternoon. The voices of boys hidden in the branches, the low rumble as somebody emptied his bucket into a box, and Mr. Taber cautioning, "Easy now! Easy! Don't bruise them apples . . . bruise them apples."

It was almost dark as I climbed the hill alone to the dining hall. The perfume of apples still hung around me, and my hands felt rough and dry, like the hands of someone much older. It was the last day of my childhood, the first of my life in New England. I've lived here, on the edge of the woods, ever since. And as Robert Frost says of earth and love, I don't know where it's likely to go better.

The Old Canoe

ella called me from the Adirondacks a week or so ago; wanted to know if I had the time to sand and varnish and paint an old canoe. Well, I don't; but it's the kind of thing you can do evenings, and I do love old canoes. So I told him to bring it on over.

It was a beauty, all right: still had the little diamond-headed brass thwart bolts along the gunwales, brass rub strips, and the old-fashioned floppy rings in the decks for attaching lines. Its seats had been re-caned, but by an expert with the right kind of cane, not some dubber. If its owner had brought me a Stradivarius, I'd have felt no more reverent about it as we unloaded it. This canoe had obviously lived in some beautiful places, and had made them more beautiful by being there.

But there was something else about it—something familiar, like a voice from long ago, or the pattern of trees against the sky outside my bedroom window. The canvas was painted green, but I had a feeling that it ought to be dark blue. The old spar varnish inside was dark and a little too thick, and looked as though it might have been put on by an impatient young varnisher just learning his trade. Unless I missed my guess, if I looked up under the forward deck, where the ribs came almost together, I'd find where the varnish had run and beaded, and not been sanded smooth. And while I was up there, if I looked up underneath at the brass bolt coming through the deck, I'd find where that same novice, having carelessly lost the original hexagonal brass nut, had substituted a square, nickel-plated steel one. I was right: The varnish was beaded, and the rusty old nut was still there, where I had tightened it, clumsily, with a pair of pliers, in 1956.

This was the first job I had ever worked on alone. Even with that qualification, it was embarrassing. It was like meeting a girl I had danced with in, say, the seventh grade, and stepped all over her feet. She was just as beautiful now as she'd been then; but now she seemed more beautiful. We were both much older, and the eye of the beholder saw much more. I picked at the flakes of paint with my thumbnail. "Well, sweetheart," I muttered, "I dubbed it up in good shape the first time, but here's a second chance, and probably the last. Let's get it right this time."

This was also the canoe that figured in one of the adventures of my youth—the very day after I had finished varnishing it. She had belonged then to a family of wealthy summer folks for whom I guided, paddling one or two of them around a private club lake while they flailed at the water with their floppy 19th-century bamboo fly rods and long strings of dropper flies. Many the time I had sat in that caned rear seat, ducking their wayward casts or carefully picking a mess of Parmachenee Belles and Royal Coachmen from my hat and shirt. On moonlit nights they liked to go out for paddles with a guitar and sing old songs like "It's a Long Way to Tipperary" or "Pack up Your Troubles."

The family I guided for was the Woodruffs. The old man's name was Willard Woodruff. (That's not his real name; but it's close enough so that I can see him clearly enough to tell the story right, and far away enough to avoid a libel suit.) He was a grim old captain of American industry, the son of a robber baron. After he'd had a few drinks, he often swore that if Franklin Roosevelt had ever appeared between the headlights of his Packard on a dark night, he would have been the late Franklin Roosevelt sooner than he had been. And Willard Woodruff's chauffeur would have gotten a hefty raise.

His son's name was the same as his, but, though the son was over sixty, all his friends called him "Junior." He was pretty goofy—he'd never had to be anything else—and he had terrible trouble pronouncing consonants, which didn't help his image any. He was terribly shy, for which—all things considered—he certainly could be forgiven. Whenever folks from nearby camps came over in the evenings for drinks, he just kind of stood there staring at the women, while his old man blustered and roared and generally bullied everybody in sight. "Junior!" he'd holler. "We need some more ice here!" That was my job, not Junior's; but he always came running into the kitchen with the ice bucket and did it.

The day I varnished the old canoe was warm and sunny. I was down on the dock, slathering it on, when Charlie, one of the old guides from across the lake, came over to see me. "Will," he said, "I got a problem over t' my place. Maybe you could come over tomorrow night and help me out." His voice had an undercurrent of excitement in it. So of course I went over the next night, as soon as my dishes were done.

Traditional Adirondack camps were never just one building. There were kitchen/dining room buildings; sleeping buildings; living rooms and dressing rooms; often as many as two dozen scattered through the woods. Charlie and I went up to his guide camp. He poured me a shot of bourbon and told me about his problem. "I think I've got a peeping Tom over here," he said. "The women tell me they're sure somebody's spying on their lean-to when they go up to bed at night. So here's what I want you to do. You get down by the dock and kind of lay low. If a canoe or a guide boat comes in, wait till whoever's in it leaves, and then take the paddles or the oars out. Be sure you get 'em all. And then wait and see what happens."

It was deathly still, except for a few crickets and bullfrogs. I hadn't been there twenty minutes when I heard a canoe bump softly against the dock. Somebody got out, pulled it up a little, and tiptoed up the path in the dark. I slipped down, took out the paddle, and hid in the bushes again. The smell of fresh varnish hung heavy in the air.

All at once there was the most tremendous BOOM! I'd ever heard. It lifted me right up off the ground. About the time my mind recognized old Charlie's 12-gauge, I heard running footsteps coming back down the path, and someone muttering, "O by Dod! O by Dod!" He pushed off the canoe and jumped in, and I could hear him scratching for the paddle. Then I heard birdshot pattering down on the leaves and plooping into the lake. The unseen man in the canoe was panicked, almost in tears. There was an odd splashing sound, like a swimming dog, paddling off into the dark.

Well, last week I was running an emery board down through the drain holes in the gunwales of that lovely old canoe, and I thought about that night, so long ago. Just then the emery board struck something lumpy between the ribs. I poked at it. A little bead of #6 shot, stuck in that goopy coat of varnish for almost forty years, rolled down into the flat of the hull. It's in my dresser right now, in my grandfather's collar-button box, along with all my other treasured souvenirs.

Favor Johnson

now was falling softly past the street lamps in the village, muffling the sounds of the occasional car and the rattle of the brook down behind the post office and the general store. It was just past suppertime, and folks were settled in for the evening. From almost every chimney, smoke drifted up through the falling snow. A few houses were hung with wreaths and colored lights around the front doors. Through the front windows gleamed lights on Christmas trees.

Just after seven o'clock, a pair of shaky headlights came slowly down the Three Mile Road, and an old blue pickup truck puttered into the light of the street lamps. The truck stopped at the first house. A man in overalls and rubber boots got out, reached back into the front seat for a small package, and trudged up through the snow to the kitchen door of the house. He knocked, the door opened, and he went inside. A few minutes later he came back out again, with the sound of voices following him. "Merry Christmas!" someone called, and he waved.

He got back into his truck, drove to the next house, and repeated the routine. Then to the next, and the next, all the way down through the village. At some houses he stopped briefly, at others quite a few minutes. Shortly after ten, having visited them all, he turned the old truck around, drove back up through the village, and disappeared into the night, his single red taillight glowing dimly through the snow. Favor Johnson had delivered his Christmas presents again.

In every house where he'd stopped, there was now a small cylindrical package wrapped in aluminum foil and decorated with the Christmas seals that come in the mail. When these packages were unwrapped later, they would reveal tin cans with one end removed and a fruitcake baked inside. For single folks and couples, it was a soup can; for families of up to five, a vegetable can; and for larger establishments, a tomato can—all of them full to the brim with the most succulent fruitcake you could imagine. Mixed up with homemade butter and studded with hickory nuts, candied cherries and pineapple, citron, raisins, and currants, it was flavored with Favor's own hard cider. Parents often would use that as an excuse to keep kids from eating more than their share of it.

Where old Favor had paused only momentarily or gone only as far as the doorstep, there remained the scuff marks of his boots in the snow, where he'd shuffled his feet nervously. But where he'd gone inside and chatted, or perhaps shared a bit of cheer, the distinctive odor of cow barn lingered faintly in the air, a further reminder of who had brought the foil-wrapped package for which each family was already making its special plans. And always some child would ask, "Why did Mr. Johnson bring us a fruitcake?"

"Well," a mother or father would answer, "it's just his way of saying 'Merry Christmas.'"

"Does he do it every year?"

"Yep."

"Does he take one to everybody in the village?"

"Yep."

"Has he always done it?"

Well, no he hadn't. And so the story of Favor Johnson and the flatlander doctor and the origin of the fruitcake would be told again.

Favor and his sister Grace had been twins, the only children of a hardscrabble farmer and his wife a couple of miles above the village. They'd gotten their names from an old Baptist hymnbook. Leafing through it for inspiration, their mother had come across the hymn "Praise, My Soul, the King of Heaven," and had been struck by the line, "Praise Him for His grace and favor to our fathers in distress." So Grace and Favor it had been.

When the old folks gave up farming, during the thirties, they stayed on in the house and split the farm between the kids. Grace and her husband built a small house on their half, and Favor, a bachelor, lived with the old folks.

When the Second World War began, the Army said that Favor was too old to fight, but they made him a cook. He'd never cooked before in his life, but much to everybody's surprise, he turned out to have a talent for it. He became mildly famous in his outfit, even when they were in combat in France. Staff officers were forever commandeering him for their special dinners.

When Favor came home from the war in 1945 he took up farming again, and surprised everybody by marrying and starting a family. But his wife's health wasn't robust, so the one child, a daughter, was all they ever had. About the time the daughter graduated from high school, Favor's wife died. The daughter married, moved far away, and failed to keep in touch. Grace and her husband sold their half of the farm to a young couple and moved south. The old folks had died during the war. So Favor was left alone.

The yard and the house slowly grew shabby, the barn ramshackle. Favor sold most of the stock, keeping only two or three milkers. He ran a few chickens and a couple of pigs, kept a horse to haul firewood, and did a little sugaring in the spring. He must have had forty cats around the place, and one dog, his constant companion, a spotted hound named Hercules. Favor kept pretty much to himself and rarely had occasion to speak—except, perhaps, to Hercules.

And then one spring the town fathers decreed a reassessment of all town property, and suddenly Favor's farm was worth a lot more money. His taxes went up far beyond his meager means. So he decided to sell his view. Above his house was a ten-acre field, and the view from the top to the south and west was magnificent. You could see all the way from Ascutney in the south to Killington and Camels Hump in the west. And on a clear winter day, you could even see the round, snowy hump of Giant Mountain, way over in New York. Real estate agents had pestered him for years to let them sell that view. Now at last he had to.

The field was bought by a wealthy surgeon from a big hospital in Massachusetts, a Dr. Jennings. The doctor and his wife hired a fancy architect, and the next summer Favor's field was capped by a magnificent, glass-fronted weekend home where the Jenningses said they hoped to retire someday. The Jenningses were good people, solid and predictable. Favor would hear their Mercedes diesel coming up the road almost every Friday evening, then roar as Doc downshifted for the driveway up to the house in the field. They'd stay till Sunday afternoon and then go back home for the week. Saturday mornings, Doc Jennings would wander down to Favor's yard to chat, buy eggs or milk, or talk about mowing the field. He often invited Favor up to the house for a drink or a cup of coffee. Favor was always polite, even pleasant, but he never went. When they left him little gifts now and then on holidays, he was always embarrassed by them, and sometimes even threw them away rather than use them.

One early winter afternoon—on a Christmas Eve—Hercules failed for the first time in his life to show up at the barn door during the evening milking. Concerned, Favor went to the door and called and whistled. No Hercules. Then Favor remembered that he'd heard rabbit hunters in his swamp that afternoon. So after milking he took a flashlight and started for the swamp. It was dark and beginning to snow. As he headed down the hill, he heard Doc Jennings downshift for the driveway, and remembered that it was Friday.

Hours later, after wandering all through the swamp calling for his dog, he heard a whine coming from a tangle of alders, and found Hercules. He'd been shot. One side of his head and a shoulder were badly torn up, and he'd bled a lot onto the snow. Favor scooped him up and headed back toward the house, stumbling in the thick brush. His flashlight finally faded and died. Just as he scrambled up onto the shoulder of the road with the dying dog in his arms, he heard the sound of the big turbodiesel coming, and the lights of Doc's car swept across him. The car skidded to a stop in the gravel and Doc jumped out. "My god!" he cried. "What's happened?"

Favor told him.

"Come on!" said Doc. "I've got a blanket in the back. Let's wrap him up and get him to a vet!"

"Nope," said Favor. "I don't want to do that. He don't look like he's gonna live, and this is the only home he's ever known. If he's gonna die, it ought to be right here." Tears mingled with the sweat on Favor's red face.

"All right," answered Doc. He shouted back into the car. "Honey, run back up to the house and get that first aid kit in the kitchen. Come on, Favor, let's get that dog in the house!"

Doc was all dressed up in a three-piece suit. He and his wife had been headed for the midnight church service. But as he and Favor entered the kitchen, he threw his suitcoat over a chair. He rolled up his sleeves, told Favor to put Hercules onto the porcelain-topped table, and began to examine the weakly panting dog. "Heat some water, will you?" he asked. "And I'll need a candle and a sharp knife, some tweezers if you've got 'em, and a pair of sharp-nosed pliers." In a few minutes Mrs. Jennings came back with the first aid kit. Doc told her to go on to church, but on the way back to stop at the hospital emergency room and pick up some things he'd order by phone. She left, and he and Favor went back to work on old Hercules.

His jaw was broken. Some teeth were missing. One shoulder had been torn open by the blast and the flesh was full of shot. He was too weak to struggle. He only moaned as Doc, whose sensitive fingers had probed the tissues of the rich and famous, worked on him under the flickering fluorescent kitchen fixture.

"I don't know if it's proper to pray for a dog, Favor," he said, "but it can't hurt. This old guy's not in very good shape."

About one in the morning Mrs. Jennings brought the supplies Doc had ordered over the phone. She brewed coffee and heated some sweet rolls she'd bought at an all-night convenience store in town. About three o'clock Doc finally took his last stitch, swabbed the wounds with antiseptic one last time, and gave the exhausted dog a shot for the pain. He and Favor lifted him gently and laid him on his mat beside the kitchen stove.

"That's all I can do," he said, washing his hands at the kitchen sink. "Now we'll have to wait and see."

"Thanks, Doc," said Favor. "He sure looks a lot better'n he did. What do I owe you?"

Doc Jennings put both hands on Favor's shoulders. His own shoulders sagged with weariness, and his eyes were moist.

"Owe me? Why, nothing, Favor. There's little enough you and I can do for each other, and this was the most, I guess, that I can do for you. I know you'd do whatever you could for me if I ever needed it. I'll be down around ten to take a look at Hercules. You'd better get some sleep. Oh! I almost forgot. Merry Christmas!"

When Doc came down later, Hercules was too weak to raise his head in greeting. His long tail thumped softly on the mat beside the stove. He was going to be all right. Doc had brought a gift with him, a fancy, boxed fruitcake from an expensive mail-order place somewhere. Favor thanked him again for saving Hercules, and for the fruitcake. But later, tasting it for the first time, he gagged. "Pfah!" he said. "I can do better'n that!"

And that's how it started. He made just one that first year, for Doc and Mrs. Jennings, and then a few the next year for some old friends. The response was so tremendous that within just a few years his list had expanded to include the whole village.

And now the whole village responds in kind. During the two weeks of the holiday season his bedraggled dooryard is hardly ever without a visiting car or two, and his kitchen is piled high with gifts that he savors and enjoys all through the long winter. Some of the village kids even think he's Santa Claus, and that seems to give him the greatest pleasure of all.

The White-Footed Mouse

Nightfall comes early during hunting season. The shortest day of the year is only a month away. It was long after dark on a Friday evening when Charlie and I set off up the woods road that led to his camp on the mountain. The wind had backed around to the north during the day, and with the setting of the sun the air had turned bitter cold. By reflected starlight, we crunched over a fresh crust of snow. On the hillside below us, down toward Mossy Cascade, a tree split suddenly with a booming sound, while around our chins our breath froze white on wool coat collars. A night cold enough, Charlie's father used to say, to freeze the balls off a brass monkey.

After about half an hour the cabin loomed through the trees, dark against the hillside. The floorboards of the little porch had frozen while they were wet, and groaned loudly under our weight. We wrestled the galvanized steel porcupine shield away from the door. The padlock was frozen stiff. We heated the key with book matches and tried again. The door creaked open at last to a still, icy blackness that seemed even colder than the woods outside.

Quickly we lit a kerosene lamp, stuffed birch bark and kindling into the cookstove, and touched a match to them. The little blaze struggled against the plug of cold air in the chimney, and smoke leaked from every crack in the range. But in a minute it began to draw. The smoking stopped, and we stood together in front of the firebox, holding our hands palms down over the black iron top, pretending that we felt some warmth from it already. We luxuriated in the sights and smells of camp—birch smoke, kerosene, brown and gray wool blankets hung from the rafters, and the antlers of the huge buck that Charlie had shot his first season back from the Navy after five years away.

Charlie's camp was built in the old way: a board platform on posts, sixteen feet square, with walls studded up to six feet. A small window in each of three sides and a door in the fourth. Rafters in a pyramid, rising from the corners of the building and supporting a heavy, olive-drab canvas roof—a Korean War surplus tent. Wood range in one corner, with an old, stained porcelain sink close by, food shelves, a tin breadbox, and an old wooden cheese box for silverware. There were two-tiered bunks built into two corners, and a box stove big enough to hold a fire most of the night—but big enough, too, to drive everybody out onto the porch if the damper were carelessly left too far open. The place was lighted by kerosene lamps.

The stove at last began to throw enough heat to warm the camp. We pulled chairs up in front of the oven and sat quietly, sipping Jim Beam from porcelain coffee mugs, talking about the next morning's hunt, and listening to the crackling of the fire. Neither one of us wanted to take the axe and pail and go for water at the brook, yet one of us would have to before long. The subject hung unspoken in the air between us.

After a while, Charlie's chin dropped slowly down toward his chest, and he fell asleep. I counted the ticking of the stovepipe, and was just about to doze off myself, when a sudden, small movement caught my eye, high on the wall above the breadbox. I turned my head and saw a little white-footed mouse walking slowly along the two-by-four plate at the top of the frame wall. I know that mice usually scurry or scamper, but not this one. He was walking. He moved without hesitation, but almost as if he were stiff. No wonder. It's a miracle he wasn't frozen solid.

When Charlie's father had built the camp, years before, he had solved the problem of insulating the cookstove pipe by running it through a section of ten-inch clay sewer pipe set into the wall just below the plate. The clay pipe always got warm, but never dangerously hot. The mouse seemed to be heading right toward it.

On he came, with an occasional pause to make sure we were still in our chairs. He passed over the china shelf, the door casing, the kerosene lamp in its wall bracket, and came at last to the clay pipe above the stove. With a slow motion amazing in one so tiny, he tentatively reached out one forefoot and tested the temperature of the pipe.

He must have been satisfied there was no danger, because then he stepped down onto the pipe, settled down in the classic pose of a library lion, and wrapped his long tail around him and over his nose. All the time, his eyes never left my face. He knew that I saw him, but he didn't seem to care. Cold is a hunger that drives us to desperate actions; and the fellowship of the freezing is, paradoxically, a warm and trusting one.

So there we all sat, for the better part of an hour, enjoying the radiance of the stove and the lamp. Eventually I decided to go get the pail of water, after all. As I came back in the door with it, stamping my feet, I stood eyeball-to-eyeball with the mouse for several long moments. He sat motionless, steeped in the fumes of the whiskey on my breath. He had obviously decided that, whatever the fates accorded him in this relationship, it had to be better than freezing to death in his icy nest down behind the breadbox.

I reached into the carton of food we had carried up with us and fished out a piece of chocolate chip cookie. I set it very carefully on the clay pipe about an inch from his nose.

The last thing I saw that night, just before cupping my hand above the lamp chimney and blowing out the light, was the gleam of his little black eye up in that corner above the stove. In the morning both he and the cookie crumb were gone.

New England Reeling

The other day, when it snowed so, I was lucky enough to be working right at home, in my shop in the basement, and didn't have to go anywhere. So I just hummed merrily along down there, watching the snow stack up on the windows and slowly shut out the sky. By afternoon there'd be enough snow up in the recent logging jobs to carry me and the dog right over the catchy little stobs sticking up everywhere.

Then, just about ten o'clock, the shop radio took a station break for a brief news broadcast. Pretty serious stuff—John Wayne Bobbitt, Michael Jackson, Tonya Harding—and right at the end, a mention of the weather. "New England is reeling under the impact of blizzard conditions and record cold temperatures!" panted the announcer, and in breathless tones went on to describe how awful it was out there—trains and planes stuck or grounded, folks dropping like cluster flies on a frozen windowpane, cars stranded, homes without power. Sounded like a disaster.

"Judast!" I thought, "I'd better get out and take a look at this. Sounds like another Storm of the Century." So I put a couple more chunks of hard maple into the furnace, pulled on my shoepacs, tuque, and down jacket, called the dog, and ventured out into the williwaw.

For a disaster scene, the yard seemed strangely unruffled. Couple feet of new snow, maybe, and more coming down, but fluffy and light. Pretty cold, too—about 8 below—but a lot warmer than it had been before breakfast. Not a bad day at all for New England in January. I opened the garage door, touched off the little Toyota truck, backed it out, and headed down the driveway.

My truck is only two-wheel-drive, but in that light snow it had its feet pretty well on the ground. The main problem was seeing; the snow was coming up over the hood. The dog was pretty nervous, but I had the tires in old ruts, and we were as good as on rails. As we came around the corner at the foot of the driveway hill, I could see the town plow had left a windrow about four feet high at the road. Too late to stop, so I poured it on. Nothing coming as far as I could see.

"Hang on, Sweetie!" I cried. There was a huge, white explosion, and we were parked in the middle of the freshly-plowed road, headed right toward the village. Down at the post office, Jean was quietly poking the last of the fourth-class mail into the boxes. I peeked around the corner of the window to see if she was reeling. Nope. Same over at the store: Frank was placidly spreading mayonnaise onto a batch of ham-and-Swiss. He looked all right to me, but I thought I'd better check.

"Frank," I asked, "are you reeling from the effects of this storm?"

He looked over his shoulder. "What in hell are you talking about?"

"Uh, nothin'. Just checkin'." I got a lunch pie and left. Ascending our driveway was a little tougher than descending, and hitting the garage door opening was a bit dicey, but we made it fine. The dog stayed outside to reel around in the snow for a while; I reeled inside to give Mother her mail.

I don't know why the media people do that to us. Maybe because any story, no matter how overblown, is better than none. But all these stupendous adjectives and vivid verbs have the effect in the long run of numbing us worse than the cold might. For generations New Englanders have played the old game, "How cold 'dyou have it to your place this mornin'?" And there's no way you can improve on "thirty-four below" by shrieking about the wind chill. Most of us hereabouts can tell whether the wind's blowing. This hysterical stuff smacks of those idiot notices the government makes stove manufacturers put on their products: "Warning—May be hot when in operation."

We folks whose regional delicacy is New England boiled dinner don't need any lessons in grim reality; we've got that up to here. No matter how bad the kid standing in front of the weather map says it's going to be, we've all seen it worse at one time or another. Besides which, one reason a lot of us live here is probably that surviving and flourishing in this climate is such a good, moral thing to do. It's decadent to be warm all the time.

I like to look at those touristy calendars with full-color pictures of the beauty of this neck of the woods and count the cost of that beauty. A fly fisherman playing a trout beneath a covered bridge is surrounded (could the camera but see them) by hordes of mosquitoes and blackflies. A shot of a snow-drifted country lane makes my cracked fingers throb. Another of budding trees reminds me of having to take off my muddy shoes every time I step into the house. A flower garden—annual crops of rocks. Smoke rising from a chimney—hauling firewood.

If you live here by choice, you pay your dues, take what you can get, and endure what you have to. It's well worth it.

Whenever I hear the weather person trumpeting dangerous wind chills, I remember trudging to work one morning years ago at fifty below, looking up the mountain and seeing Harley Branch, one of our truck drivers, walking back down the road with his gear shift lever hanging from his mitten. It had snapped right off at the floor. "God, Harley!" I hollered. "You must be 'bout frozen!"

"You just wait'll I take this shiftin' lever in to the old man," he said. "It'll be right warm around here in a minute!"

The Child of Fear

I could always tell when Bernie was getting ready to ask a question. He sat in the corner, in the back seat of the row by the windows, in a desk too small for his long, slender frame. In my memory I see him always wearing blue jeans and a Lee Rider denim jacket. Behind him, out the window, the parking lot and half a dozen yellow school buses. Beyond that, the mountains rising at the edge of the valley floor.

Normally he sprawled back in his seat with his legs stuck into the aisle, squinting at me with an incredulous expression. But when he was getting ready to ask one of his questions, he leaned forward, with his knees together and bouncing up and down, elbows on the desk in front of him, and fists in front of his mouth. Then, at last, the dreaded blue denim sleeve waving in the air.

"Bernie?"

"Mr. Lange, didn't you tell us yesterday that a pronoun subject of a clause is always in the subjective case, even if the clause is the object of another clause?"

"Uh . . . yes, I think I did."

"And wasn't Alfred Lord Tennyson a famous poet? Like, probably the most famous poet in England?"

"Yes, he was poet laureate of England."

"Uh-huh. Then how come in this poem he wrote he says, '. . . and see the great Achilles, *whom* we knew'? Isn't 'whom' the objective case?"

And off we'd go, twisting through thickets of misunderstanding, scribbling sample sentences on the chalkboard. Returning to definitions to get our bearings, then starting out again, while the rest of the class rolled their eyes at each other. And when I finally got all the way through it, I'd turn to find him looking out the window at the mountains. For as soon as he'd detected that I was once more going to wiggle out of an apparent contradiction, he'd lost interest.

Or this one: "Mr. Lange, didn't you tell us that when Iago says he wishes Cassio's fingers were 'clyster pipes,' he means he wishes they were enema pipes?"

"Yeesss . . ."

"What's an enema?"

That sort of question usually brightened up the rest of the class. As they watched with fascination to see how I'd get out of this one—what euphemisms I could possibly invent to describe the operation, I would conceive the almost overwhelming urge to give Bernie a personal demonstration.

He wasn't being a smart aleck, either. I was too much bigger than he was, and pretty up-tight in those days, to boot. No, he wasn't just having fun. It was anger. You could feel the angry energy he was giving off, like static electricity. For some reason, I attracted a lot of it. And yet after class there he was, at the fringe of maybe four or five kids who stayed to talk or ask questions. Smiling uncertainly, wanting to be included, taking his cues from the others, yearning for something—like the puppy who chews up your slippers.

As far as I could tell, he had no friends among his classmates. In a very small town like that one, where everybody knows everybody else, kids are normally classmates from kindergarten right through high school. Friendships and reputations form early and tend to last, often all the way through life. And the occasional odd man out remains odd man out for life, as well.

In memory, I am looking out the teacher's room window just after three o'clock, watching the village kids head home on foot while the blatting yellow buses disperse to the rest of the township. And there is Bernie in his denim jacket and jeans, hands in his pockets, trudging alone across the trussed bridge over the millpond, past the hardware store and the liquor store, turning left at the United Church of Christ, and disappearing behind the houses on the Reber Road.

I was taking graduate courses in education up at Plattsburgh State so that I could get my permanent teacher certification. One of the things they taught us to do was make "sociograms." On the seating charts of our classes we drew solid lines between the names of students whom we knew to have close relationships, dotted lines between casual friends. I never could see the utility of it—except that it was impossible not to notice that there were no lines at all running to Bernie's seat in the back corner by the window. But I knew that already.

I didn't know what to say to him then. Nobody did. And it's too late now. God! If I could rewind thirty-five years! I'd do it differently: I'd let him catch me in a corner once or twice. I'd misuse a pronoun now and then, and hope he'd pick it up. But I was so young! It never occurred to me to wonder where his anger came from, or where it was going, or why I attracted it. I was too young then to know that anger is the child of fear. Bernie didn't know that, either. If either one of us had known it, he might still be here. He was forever punching at shadows. I'm ashamed to remember that he never laid a glove on me.

It was a clumsy, stumbling relationship. Once, before class, he brought me a photograph of a fox he'd shot. I admired it with all the enthusiasm I could muster and when the bell rang, handed it back to him. He glared at me all through class, his arms folded across his chest. As he went out, I asked, "What's the matter, Bernie? You look upset."

"That picture was a present, not just to look at!" He stomped out.

The next day, out of the blue, he asked me to go rabbit hunting with him. I have wished ever since that I hadn't said yes. And yet, I'm not so sure. Something had to happen.

He had a nice little beagle-spaniel bitch named Queenie, eleven years old, but a really good rabbit dog. And that Saturday morning she was happy as a cow in clover; there were rabbits everywhere. Toward noon she chased a cottontail through thick brush about forty yards in front of me. I had only a .22 automatic, so I was letting the rabbit go. It was too tough a shot.

"Shoot! Shoot!" cried Bernie, right beside me, and I shot, twice. The first shot pierced the rabbit through the eyes. The second shot killed Queenie, who was upon the rabbit as it fell. We ran together, wildly hoping, toward the dead rabbit and the dead dog, and stood over them. They lay side by side, warm little bodies touching each other in the relaxation of death as they never could in life. Incredulity mixed with horror, anger with understanding, and shame with pity. I don't know what we said to each other, if anything. I remember only the desperate reaching out, the groping toward each other of two young people who could reach, but not touch. In time, it might have happened. But there wasn't enough time.

We buried the dog and the rabbit side by side. We straightened to go. I put a hand on his shoulder. "Bernie," I said, " I'm sorrier about this than I can ever tell you." He shrank away from my touch, crouching. "If I were you," he snarled, "I wouldn't stand by any lighted windows after dark anymore." The next thing I remember, I was holding him up against a pine tree by his denim lapels, shaking him. His head flopped forward. His mouth gaped, and I saw thickly that someone had bloodied his nose. "I'm sorry!" he cried. "I'm sorry!" As I paused, he said quietly, "I'm sorry. I didn't think that would upset you."

Neither of us ever mentioned it again. He never asked another question in class. And I never told him how much I liked him. No one ever did. Not in language he could understand. A year later, my family and I moved away, to another job.

He graduated from high school and joined the

Marines. I saw him only once more, home from boot camp with a livid scar running from his hairline down his face and into his collar. A bayonet fight with a young black man, I was told. I didn't have to be told how it started.

A couple of months later he descended into the black hole of Viet Nam, from which, even today, almost nothing has escaped unscathed or unchanged, even the truth. Little people he couldn't see or understand—who wore no uniforms, seemed to play by no discernible rules, and refused to explain themselves—were shooting at him from the jungle. He couldn't stand that. So one last time he stood up and shook his fist at the inscrutable face of fear, and they shot him in the head. Among the stuff in his pockets when he died was a photograph, sent to him by his mother, of my wife and our new baby.

I visit him now whenever I'm in Washington, trace with my fingers the familiar letters of his name incised into the black granite wall, and realize vainly and too late: how futile it was to speak to Bernie about the cases of pronouns. What we needed—both of us—was more time. Time, and a chance to grow old enough to put a face on fear. He never got the chance.

Gals at the Bor'as

arry Perkins was his name—still is, I suppose, wherever he is today—and he'd been born solely to illustrate the meaning of the word callow. It's been around for centuries, I imagine. But it was never perfectly defined until the day Barry walked up across the lake ice one February morning in 1958 and reported to old Bill, the camp boss.

There were eight of us in camp, skidding logs down off the north slope of Pinnacle into a yard, where we bucked them up into firewood of three different lengths, for cookstoves, box stoves, and fireplaces. Then we hauled the wood to the camps around the lake and ranked it in the sheds.

It's just as Robert Frost says: Among even the most thoughtful of us, there's a difference between cutting wood for yourself and cutting it for money. Both have elements of art, science, machismo, and competition; but one emphasizes aesthetic results and the other, volume. One makes the day seem to fly by, the other to make it drag so that it seems dusk will never come—let alone even lunch.

The result of this is that woodcutters-for-hire, especially when working side by side, become fiercely (if tacitly) competitive, and build up quite a bit of aggression. Life in camp can be as tough as inside a chicken coop. But a good boss will see to it that nobody is bottom chicken. However, there are some just born to it. Barry was one of these. And when you add to that the circumstance of his entering late into a group already sorted out, you just knew that he was in for it.

Let no one tell you that woodsmen are rugged individualists. They're rugged, all right. But they have a code of dress, speech, and behavior as rigid as any convent's; and only within those regulations do individuals express their differences. With us, it was double wool socks and high rubbers; one-piece wool long johns; black wool Ballard-cloth pants; police suspenders; wool shirts, and wool or quilted vests on a cold day; cowhide choppers; and checked wool hunting shirts, usually unbuttoned, with the long tails dangling. Only in the matter of hats was individuality accepted—expected, as a matter of fact.

Into this siberian sameness Barry walked unawares, togged out in brand-new Bean boots, Lee Rider jeans, bright red down jacket with an old lift ticket attached to the zipper, downhill ski mitts, and—so help me!—a Sherlock Holmes deerstalker. We spotted him coming at lunchtime, still about a mile down the lake. "Sweet sufferin' Christ!" exclaimed old George Lamb. "What in hell is this comin'? Hand me those binoculars, will you, Billy?"

The lake was swept nearly clear of snow by the wind, and slippery, so he was sort of shuffling along, a maroon dufflebag under one arm and the other mittened hand over his nose. Every so often he'd switch hands, or stop and wave his arms around in circles to get his fingers warm. We watched him coming all through lunch. Finally he spotted the smoke in the chimney, came under the shelter of the point, and stomped up onto the porch. George opened the door, and he jammed through it, his dufflebag catching on the latch. His face was as red as his parka, with tears streaming down his cheeks, and a bright, clear pearl dripping from the end of his nose.

"You take the wrong path out of the parking lot, Sonny?" asked George. "This ain't the ski shop."

"No, sir. I'm Barry Perkins, and Mr. Branch sent me up to work."

"Work, eh? Well, by Judas, you come to the right place!"

And so he had. He didn't know a maul from an ice chisel, or a peavey from a flat file. But he was bright, willing, and good-natured; and the old-timers don't require any more of their help than that. After the first full day of work, he fell asleep at the table. But in less than a week, he was sitting around with the rest of us after supper, till bedtime, or in the easy chair by the gas lamp, looking at old copies of *Playboy*.

We'd been there two weeks, and were all getting a little eager to get to town again, when one Saturday just before supper Roger Benoit said, "Boy! If I was young again, I'd sure as hell take 'er for the Bor'as tonight!" We all nodded knowingly in assent. "What's the Bor'as?" asked Barry.

"Why, it's a dance hall, boy, with a band and everythin' on Saturday night, and lots of girls. But it's quite a walk from here, right up through the woods and a hell of a frozen swamp." It was, too—

about twelve miles over a height of land into the Boreas Ponds and the Hudson River watershed. There was nothing there, of course—never had been—but ponds, swamps, and snow. Oh, a hotel once, I guess, but about a hundred years ago.

Well, the longer Barry thought about that dance hall and all those women up there, the more excited you could see he was getting. It was really cold outside—damn near zero—but he was hot as a firecracker. Forty minutes later, armed with my compass, George's snowshoes, Bill's flashlight and extra batteries, and a bag of cold cornbread, off he went into the icy darkness.

We figured he'd be back around breakfast time, all frustrated. We'd listen to his story and tell him where he made the wrong turns. Maybe we could even get him to try again the following week. After all, he'd already been willing to walk all the way down the lake one evening to look for a spare chainsaw battery at the lower boathouse.

But he didn't return Sunday morning, or all that day. As darkness fell Sunday evening, he was very much on our minds. "He isn't back by breakfast, Roger," said old Bill, "you're gonna take a little stroll up to the Bor'as. 'Twas your goddamned idea. It's gonna snow tomorrow, and I think that boy is in some trouble."

He came in before dawn Monday morning, just as old George lit the kerosene-soaked kindling in the cookstove. Without a word, he picked up the empty water bucket and ice chisel and headed down to the lake for water. The rest of us were getting up when he came stamping back in.

"Where the hell you been, boy?" asked Bill.

"Up t'the Bor'as."

"How was it?"

"Great! Just as good's you said it was. Maybe even better."

Well, that was the last time anybody mentioned it. Nor could you ever have referred to Barry again as callow. He was now . . . well, whatever the cat is after it's swallowed the canary; that's what he was. And there was definitely—I stopped several times to sniff it myself—there was clearly an aroma of cheap perfume hanging in the air around his bunk.

The Old Man's Legacy

*T*he day before Thanksgiving. A day of waiting. All the last tasks of autumn have been
completed: the garden is mulched, the firewood is under cover, the canoe is stored away in the
loft of the barn. A last wavering wedge of geese flew
over the house about a week ago. Now we wait—we,
the house, and the land—for the first snows of winter.

Down in White River and Lebanon, parents are
waiting for their kids' planes and buses to come in.
Tomorrow morning the house will slowly fill with
the aroma of roasting turkey. We will sit at the
kitchen table through the day, catching up on the
events of our lives, eating sparingly, still waiting.
Waiting for dinnertime, with its old family ritual:
Going around the table, each of us will tell what the
past year has brought him for which he is especially
thankful.

Has it really been forty years since we were the
kids getting off the buses on Wednesday night? Has
it really been thirty years since I first started spending
Thanksgiving weekend with the old man and his
boys on Giant Mountain? Was it only three years ago
that the old man and I hunted up the oak ridge
together for the last time? And is that really my

infant son down in the kitchen, loading up the pack-baskets and taking most of my load into his with a patronizing wink and a reference to my growing infirmity? How could so many autumns, so many Thanksgivings, have spun by without my noticing? They all seem to run together; yet each is as distinct as a gem in a solitaire setting, becoming more precious with each passing year.

For years we have eaten our Thanksgiving dinner together as a family. Then on the following day my son and I have gone off to the hunting camp on Giant. The ritual is as unvarying as it is cherished: through Bethel at dusk, up Rochester Mountain and down the other side; turn left at Hancock with the aroma of the UCC Church Supper blowing in through the truck heater. After Middlebury, like a spaceship leaving the earth's gravitational field, we begin to feel more there than here, and we can begin to see the loom of mountains to the west of us, on the other side of Lake Champlain. Another half-hour of driving toward the Big Dipper, fifteen minutes in four-wheel drive up the woods road, and at last we can see the lights of camp shining through the bare hardwoods. Then the voices, the handshakes and greetings unchanged, yet never the same. And this year one face and one voice missing.

The old man had been slowing down for years, of course; haven't we all? But last fall he had suddenly looked more than just older. He had looked tired, and I saw him watching and listening, instead of leading the conversation, as he always had as long as I had known him. He almost seemed to be trying to fix things in his memory, like a man filling his canteen at a stream before setting out across dry country. And toward the end of the evening, he turned to me while everybody else was talking, and said, "Will, I want you to let that boy of yours hunt with Charlie and the others tomorrow morning. I've got something I want you to help me carry."

The hunters left camp just before dawn to begin the hunts across the mountainside. The old man and I left about an hour later, just as the light of the rising sun caught the ledges of Spotted Mountain to the west. The old man carried his rifle—not the scope-mounted beauty his boys had given him, but his ancient Savage .300, from his days as a meat hunter during the Depression—and I carried, besides my own rifle, his packbasket, which he had filled with an extra wool frock, a down sleeping bag, a poncho, and some food.

We followed the old logging road behind camp to an oak-studded ridge that over the years had produced dozens of the antler racks that adorned the walls of the camp.

How the old man had slowed down! He had always been a very slow still hunter—though deadly—but this wasn't hunting. He was really working to make his way up through the dead leaves and windfalls to the ridge. And I noticed that he was doing the same thing he'd done the night before, though this time with his eyes: recording everything and filing it away in his memory. Every time he stopped to look at something, I followed his gaze, and I began to see the forest as I had never seen it before. It was almost as if he were giving it to me.

There were stacks of tanbark, stripped from hemlock logs during the winter of 1923, left there by the loggers and never picked up. Here was a scattering of wood chips dropped from the fresh workings of a pileated woodpecker. In the shade of a rotting log lay a maple leaf curled up into a cup and filled with snow, with a single beechnut resting in the white powder like a chocolate drop.

We sat on a flat, moss-covered rock and ate our lunch, watching a downy woodpecker softly working on a nearby tree. A weasel, half turned to white by the coming winter, hunted mice among the rustling brown leaves. Following the old man's eyes, I saw that every one of the beeches around us was scratched and scarred by the claws of bears climbing the trees to get the nuts before they were ready to drop. A flock of chickadees, feeding through the undergrowth, suddenly surrounded us and were just as quickly gone, their quiet comic conversation fading away up the hill.

We reached the crest of the oak ridge about the middle of the afternoon. "Now," said the old man, "I want you to leave me the packbasket and go on back down to camp. I spent the night here once as a boy about sixty-five years ago, and I've wanted to do it again ever since."

He faced down the ridge, toward the bright, sinking sun. The rattle of a brook far below us carried up the hill in the hush of the afternoon. Somewhere a jay screamed. The old man's eyes were moist. "This is the last time, you know," he said, more to himself than to me. Then he looked up. "You tell the boys not to worry. I'll be just fine. Come on up to get me around eight o'clock tomorrow morning."

I promised that I would. We sat together in the sun for a few minutes, sharing some sausage and cheese that the old man carved with his pocketknife. Then I picked up my rifle and scuffled off down the ridge, leaving him there alone. When I looked back, once, he was down on his hands and knees like an old bear, pulling together a pile of oak leaves for an easy chair in a hollow beside a big rock.

The next morning we met him coming down off the hill with the packbasket on his back and a quiet smile on his face. He stopped and looked back over his shoulder up the slope. "Well, boys," he said, "that was lovely. But it's all yours now. I'm all done. God knows I'll probably never see this hill again."

And he didn't. He did come up to camp once more, just before Christmas, but that was the end of it. In the early spring he awoke one night with his heart pounding in his chest, and within an hour he was gone. In a dark suit, instead of hunting clothes, I drove the familiar route over the mountains by daylight, and we laid him to rest on Sand Hill, where he can gaze forever across his valley and up to the peaks of the Great Range beyond.

Things will be a lot quieter this year, and the cooking will certainly be a lot less spectacular. For the first time, I'll be the oldest man in camp, and my son will be carrying most of my pack. For the first time, I'll be thinking about the day, perhaps thirty— perhaps twenty—years away, when I give my boy whatever I have left of what the old man gave me our last Thanksgiving weekend together.

Daddy and the Fawn

As sugaring season winds down each year, I always think of this old line of verse: ". . . as full of sun as a south slope in April." Driving the interstate the other day, I saw dozens of deer on the north side of the highway, basking in the warmth and nibbling the first shoots of green at the edge of the woods. The gravid does moved stiffly, looking like furry water balloons. In a couple of weeks they'll disappear to have their fawns.

Back home, this was always the difficult time between winter work and summer work, when we were hard put to keep the money coming in until the season began. But a man who really wanted to could usually find firewood to split for summer folks, or windows to wash and sashes to paint, or winter wrack to rake from yards.

For some years in April I went into camp with a crew of men to split and rank stovewood at half a dozen summer cottages. There were two lakes to cross. They were always still frozen, but deeply candled by the spring sun; so we towed guide boats behind us across the ice to make sure we could get back out, even if it melted. Those were good times— good, sweet-smelling blocks of maple, beech, and birch rising in piles beside us; good men to work with, good cooking, good stories after supper. The nights were cold and frosty, and the days warm with the promise of summer.

There were several half-tame deer who came into the yard of the camp, to scoff up the leftover cornbread the cook threw out there. There were three generations of one family of them: Fanny, an old doe; Susie, her daughter; and Mike, a little buck fawn of Susie's. Homer Brown, an old guide with a gift for animals, could feed Fanny right out of his hand, and once even enticed her into the kitchen for a biscuit. I can still see her long neck stretching out toward his hand and hear her little hoofed feet tapping and slipping on the oiled wood floor.

Baddy Bigelow was the cook, and, God! he was a good one. He was an old bachelor, and he'd been cooking for himself and his summer folks all his adult life. On the wood cookstove at camp he could make a pot roast that melted in your mouth, with gravy and potatoes and creamed onions that almost made you cry with joy. His pancakes and cherry pies seemed to evaporate before they reached the table. The boss never had trouble finding men to go to the lakes to split wood as long as Baddy was cooking.

I'd been to his house for supper a couple of times down in town. It was definitely bachelor's hall—dark brown, stained wallpaper; no curtains on the windows; linoleum wearing through to the brown in front of the stove and sink; checkered oilcloth on the table. And everywhere, pictures and trophies. Old photographs of half a dozen men with rifles standing in front of a buck pole hung with deer. Deer's feet made into coat hooks and gun racks. Great, antlered heads, imperfectly mounted, on almost all the walls. As far as I knew, Baddy wasn't a hunter. And yet there he was, as a much younger man, in almost every picture.

One evening after supper in camp, everybody hiked up to the inlet to fish at the edge of the ice. I stayed behind to help Baddy with the dishes. The deer were foraging in the yard, and we watched them as we worked. Lovely as they were, they always reminded me of hunting season.

"You don't hunt, do you, Baddy?" I asked him.

He shook his head. "Huh-uh."

"Why not? Used to, didn't you?"

"Eyah. But I ain't hunted since the spring of 1946." He looked out the window toward the frozen lake and the mountains beyond. "I hunted that first fall after I come back from Europe.

"But that next spring—'twas just about this time of year, with snow still in the woods—I was out in the back yard splittin' wood, and I heard a hell of a racket up on the hill behind my place. And when I got up there, there was three dogs had a doe down, and they had 'er all tore up.

"I had my axe in my hand, and I chased 'em off. She was still alive, but they'd pulled her inwards right out onto the snow. It was an awful thing, boy! So I brained her. And then I see somethin' still movin', and by god, it was her fawn, which was prob'ly what they was after.

"I pulled him out of there and brought him down to the house—a little buck fawn—and I cleaned him up best I could. Wrapped him up good, warmed him up some milk, and got an empty medicine bottle and wrapped an old rag around the top for him to suck on. It worked pretty good, too. He seemed to know what to do with it.

"Well, I nursed that little fella all that afternoon, and all night, too. I talked to him, and kind of encouraged him, you know, and I thought for a while there he was gonna make it. But he wan't quite ready to be born yet. 'Bout daylight he just kind of petered out.

"I buried him out by the barn, and then I set on that chopping block out there by the woodshed for a long time. I thought of all I'd done in the war, and of all the animals I'd killed in my time, and all to once I just decided that was enough. And I ain't touched any of my guns since then, except to dust 'em."

He'd been gazing out the window as he talked, and suddenly seemed startled to have said so much. Without looking at me, he walked out onto the porch and into the yard. Fanny raised her head and looked at him. They stood looking at each other until, nervous, she bobbed her head once, switched her tail, and stepped quietly back into the trees.

All Gone Away

Many people new to this part of the country are unaware of the history lying, literally, beneath their feet everywhere they tread. They see the thick trees spreading to the mountaintops and think themselves in the forest primeval. But people in their seventies and older can remember when most of that was open grazing and farm land, newly going to seed—when they could still hear their neighbors calling their cows or their hired man, and the cries of roosters echoed on the hillsides each morning.

Not any more. Plantations and second growth have reclaimed the fields, and hard times have taken the farmers. We've still got one rooster in the neighborhood, but the early-morning sound these days is mostly from the tires of imported cars as the commuters head to town.

The dog doesn't care much about history. All she knows is that, winter or summer, when the sun is westering, it's time to go for a walk. And she sits there watching me with impossibly brown eyes until I agree. This is a good time, between the last of the snow and the first of the flies: firewood-cutting season, still pleasantly cool, and we can see a long way through the woods. The budding soft maples have tinged the air with dark red, the color of a faint beet juice stain on a white tablecloth. A good time to follow old stone walls and look for old cellar holes and springs.

We followed an overgrown road, cut into the south side of a valley just above the spring high-water mark. It was a new one for us. Must have been a farm road. I tried to imagine where, out there in the silent woods, the homestead would have been. Guessing it would be on a south slope not far from a swale, I slopped through the brook and began to angle up the opposite side of the valley. I heard sounds of distress from behind me; but just as I turned back to get her, the dog found a downed tree and crossed on the trunk.

Very quiet here. Cut off by the shoulder of a hill from the sounds of the main valley, it could have been thirty miles from town. Soft maple, beech, and oak, with a scattering of white pines and hemlocks. A little beech, no higher than my chest, had finally dropped its leaves in expectation of spring. They lay in a bright copper circle around its feet. A few hepatica showed white and purple just above the duff. Very quiet. But you could sense a presence here.

Then we came across a parallel pair of stone walls and a double row of old sugar maples. The stones were rough, angular granite, the size of wheelbarrows. It cost many a blood blister and blackfly bite to worry them out of the fields and stack them here like this—to slide them up the straining planks, to pry them up with forged iron bars while sticking in the shims to steady them. We trudged between the walls a hundred yards or so, and there it was: two clumps of lilacs gone wild and rank on either side of a cut granite step. A tumbledown cellar hole lined with boulders and rubble, forty-year-old popples growing from its floor, and the twisted remains of a rusted old bedstead half buried in dead leaves.

Out back, the overgrown remains of a dooryard orchard, a rough stone springhouse, and a few iris coming up through the leaves. A pile of gray boards where a tool shed died. An aging red oak with the remains of a tree house between two horizontal branches. The privy and dump would be over here, I reckoned. We shuffled through dead oak leaves down the hill and found the dump in a hole below a moss-covered ledge.

Lots of bottles. Galvanized one-gallon kerosene can with the bottom rusted out. Fender from some vehicle. Pair of scissors rusted forever into a Saint Peter's cross. And a strangely familiar half-cylinder of stamped metal, about eight inches long, and streamlined. A piece of lettered aluminum on each side, with three letters still visible on one: COM. I'd had one just like it as a kid. It was a toy train, with the engine named "Commodore Vanderbilt." But mine had been electric. This one had an extra hole in the side for a winding key.

It was hard to imagine all that activity ever happening here—milking, haying, sugaring, washing, ironing—and the wind-up toy train going round and round by kerosene light on winter nights. And finally being discarded as the boy grew up or the family moved away.

The waxing moon shone through the bare trees. Time to go. The dog and I sat side by side on the mossy ledge. The spirit of the lost boy was still very much in that place. I left the locomotive there for it to play with.

Kids on the Sideboard

'*ve* heard it said that many people get their ideas of what God is like from what their fathers are like. From what I've seen of life, I'd have to say that's true to some extent. Certainly, my own evolving concept of God has to a surprising extent coincided with my evolving relationship with my father. And it may also help to explain why, in these days of burgeoning single parenthood, there are so many atheists around.

Out here in Etna, it's just after breakfast, around 6:40. The dishes are piled in the sink, and the phone hasn't started to ring yet. Mother and I are seated at the dining room table for our daily study and quiet time.

(Lest you think this a custom of religious long standing, I'll admit it's only two weeks old. We used to do it, many years ago, when the kids were fidgety-young, and resumed it only after our visit, a couple of weeks ago, with an elderly couple living alone on a ranch in the hills of West Texas. They seemed to derive so much of their focus and joy from their own daily contemplation that we decided we wanted some of that, too.)

It's a beautiful morning, the sun already over the hill and filtering through the leafing trees and dining room window. Cool and clear, perfect weather for working outdoors; I wish spring-feverishly that I could do all my summer's work—especially the roofs—in this one day and take the rest of May, June, and July off, till the start of my vacation. I will not, however, voice this wish aloud. Such fantasy, uttered in the midst of our busiest time of year, would make, as Shakespeare says, an unquiet house.

Well, we read a little from the second letter of Peter, and a couple of paragraphs of commentary. Then we sat quietly, while the shadows of infant maple leaves danced on the table between us. Mother spoke first. "Let's just think about the kids this morning."

She didn't realize it, but I had the advantage of her there. Right behind her and over her shoulder, the portraits of all three of our kids—two girls and a boy, now two women and a man—were lined up on the sideboard, along with several wedding pictures and a trio of grandchildren. The arrangement is Mother's work; and it came to me all at once that this was the first time I had ever really looked at it.

As a kid myself in grade school, I had to memorize great chunks of Longfellow, a misguided teacher's favorite poet. Yet bits of all those verses—"Hiawatha", "Paul Revere," the banner with the strange device, and the arrow shot into the air—linger with me still. And looking at those portraits of the three kids, so very clearly our kids, and yet so very different from each other, reminded me of the three little girls coming down from the nursery for children's hour: "Grave Alice, and laughing Allegra, and Edith with golden hair."

Sitting here in Great-Grandma Lange's creaking cane-bottom chair, steam from my coffee cup rising in a sunbeam, a few days before my sixtieth birthday, I remember that our oldest—our own "grave Alice"—had her thirty-fifth birthday only two weeks ago. She came to us on a lovely May afternoon, with the snowbanks still high beside the Adirondack roads and robins hopping on the hospital lawn. Those were still the Dark Ages, so I couldn't see her born, but sitting on the front porch, I could hear it all, including her first cries. Life suddenly got a lot more serious. It was, I reflected at the time, like being in a fight that you had expected to win and realizing with a certain anxiety that the other guy wasn't going to quit.

She was quiet, self-contained. She could sit for hours in a cardboard carton and amuse herself with almost nothing. She cried sometimes to get back into her playpen. Early on, she kept things to herself. When we finished reading the last heartbreaking paragraph of Farley Mowat's *The Dog Who Wouldn't Be*, her brother and I sobbed; she could not. In her photograph—a beautiful, long-haired woman smiling at me from behind Mother's shoulder—she is still inside her face, looking out, watching.

Her brother, just two years later, contained nothing. He shattered all our illusions that we were accomplished parents. He also shattered my Beetle's windshield with his toy hammer, which ever after was called his "no-no." Both his mother and I encouraged him to be a little man. I wish now that we hadn't. His photograph, which does not make eye contact, as his sisters' do, is of a serious young officer in uniform, still eager to please.

Seven years' break, and here came the baby, the only one of our children unlike either of her parents. The interior of a playpen was not her thing; if it ever contained her more than five minutes, I'm not aware of it. She ate everything not nailed down or locked up, went fishing with me and caught five times as many fish as I did, played Yahtzee and rolled whatever numbers she needed. Two weeks ago she finished ten quilts for the children of Oklahoma City who lost parents in the bombing. Her photograph—she has a standing love affair with cameras—smiles right at me and reminds me of her yearbook quotation, a line from *Cheers* about loving a little place "where everybody knows your name."

Of all the jobs we do in our lives, the most important is the one for which we have no experience. You couldn't get a job driving a truck with as few qualifications as we have for parenthood, and you could never keep any job if you made as many mistakes as we do raising our kids.

The biggest mistake was somehow ever letting them believe for a minute that they were valued for what they did rather than for what they were. I hope it's not too late to show them what I've recently learned about God and fathers: that, of course, we like to be proud of our children, and things they do can cause us pain. But nothing they do can make us love them more or less. There could not possibly be room for the one, or capacity for the other.

Sliding on a Shovel

omantic idylls all have their price. Most of us who are old enough to have achieved and experienced one or more of them know that. A sailing cruise of the Caribbean, for example, with the warm trade winds caressing your face all day, inevitably comes to that midnight crisis when, the wind shifting and rising, the anchor drags, and it's all hands turn to. A romantic summer getaway to the dramatic wilds of Alaska will invariably involve inhaling several hundred mosquitoes each day as they swarm around your facial orifices. And a lazy winter weekend afternoon during the January thaw here in the Currier and Ives part of New England always seems to find the weakest spot in one of your roof valleys, announcing its success by spreading a wet stain across the plaster.

Thus it was that on an otherwise lovely day I found myself standing in the rain at the top of a 12-foot ladder wielding a long-handled aluminum roof rake. The yard-deep drift in the valley above me was crusted over and soaked through. It resisted breaking, stuck to the rake whenever it could, and finally melted and ran down the handle in a drooping river. Once my mittens were good and soaked, it ran down inside the sleeves of my parka, as well. Where I leaned against the eaves waist-high, chunks of slush dripped into my trouser pockets.

But I was damned if I'd quit and retreat inside. This was just another of the little tests—sort of environmental pop quizzes—that New England throws at us every so often. Flunk more than a few and you've got to retreat all the way South, with a great echoing laugh ringing in your ears to the end of your days. So I stood grimly there till I'd reached as far as I could. I climbed down, dug the slush out of my pockets, and put away the ladder and the rake.

Then I thought, "Well, I'm wet, anyway, and not likely to get any wetter. I might's well get out the square-pointed shovel and go down and shovel out the paper tube. Plow's probably buried it, and if it freezes tonight, that bank's gonna be like iron." I took down the shovel.

I often find that folks new to the north country don't know what a square-pointed shovel is; they think it's a snow shovel. 'Tisn't. It's a scoop, shaped like a coal or grain shovel, but much shallower. It's got a long ash handle that ought to reach just about eye-high. And it's the Yankee's weapon of choice in the battle with deep and drifting snow. He'll use a snow scooter to move deposits from his dooryard out into or across the road. And now and then you might see him sort of shamefacedly utilizing an aluminum snow shovel. But that's more a woman's tool. Any old-timer who wears a hunting hat with earflaps, a blue denim frock with blanket lining, wool pants, and felt-lined galoshes always keeps a waxed long-handled shovel hanging by the door. Hanging because it's poor form to stand it where it'll leave a rusty mark when you pick it up. And waxed (with a jelly jar seal) because it'll shed snow better.

I was just about to step out the garage door when I happened to notice the condition of the dooryard and turnaround. They'd been plowed that morning. Now they were ice—smooth, gray, and hard as steel. They were also as slick and wet as a greased eel. My first step outside would be my last until I reached the road or went off into the woods. I could picture it in my mind—the lurching, stiff-legged slide, long shovel held crossways like a riverman's peavey—from the garage door downward across the turnaround, sloped to shed the rains of spring and now shedding the master of the house. I could even recite verse to give the act aesthetic context—Robert Frost's "Brown's Descent"—but that only made the picture humorous, not harmless.

And yet I would go; I do so hate to be checked by fearful considerations that would not have occurred to me when I was young. What sort of fungus is it that grows upon our consciousness in middle age and makes us begin to worry about cuts and bruises and broken bones? Surely everyone can remember the first time his doctor explained his pain to him by saying, "You're not as young as you used to be, you know."

When we were kids, they never used to salt the roads. It was sand only, and that spread by hand, too, by two men standing freezing in the back of a dump truck. Where they failed to reach, along the curb or ditch, there was room for us to "coast," they used to call it. I had a Flexible Flyer much bigger than the average run of belly-floppers, and did it fly! Pulling back on one of its two steering horns, leaning, and dragging an inside foot, I could skid around the corner at Stinard and Gordon sideways, and if I slid too far and hit the curb, I rolled into Mrs. Mahan's front yard, an unpleasant experience because of Mrs. Mahan's dog's regular habits.

That was long ago. Now, this was getting embarrassing. But suddenly I saw, as if for the first time, the shovel I was holding in my hand. Of course! Forty years ago, when I worked at the bobsled run in Lake Placid, we always came down the mountain for lunch and at quitting time on our long-handled shovels. I made sure Mother wasn't watching out the window; no sense in reinforcing her belief that I'm losing my mind. I pointed the long shovel handle downhill, sat down, and pushed off from the door jamb.

Holy Toledo! That jelly jar wax really worked! I rocketed across the turnaround, picked up the lower rut of the driveway, and shot off down the hill in a blur of ancient exhilaration. As I passed the woodpile at the bottom of the hill, my left foot caught a chunk that stuck out a little, and I whirled around, the shovel shooting out from under me. I slid into the snowbank opposite with a whump! And getting up all flushed and excited, discovered that Mrs. Mahan's dog had nothing on my neighbors' mutts.

Blood Brothers

It's just past seven in the evening, and I'm sitting by an open window, writing by daylight. Only ten weeks ago it was long dark by now, and cold, the snow in the woods glowing dully through the gloom.

But this evening I look up through green leaves at a blue sky, at light slowly turning golden as the sun drops down into the trees. What I wouldn't give to be on an orbiting space shuttle!—to see the same scene from an opposite point of view: from the blue sky looking down at the line of green advancing northward across the face of the globe, at the shadow of the earth retreating westward and the light lingering on the mountaintops.

Springtime to me used to mean *doing* things—bicycling, fishing, canoeing. Now it seems more like the fulfillment of a divine promise.

Life seems to spring perpetually from nothing. Hiking some years ago through the year-old ashes of a forest fire, I was astonished to see green shoots of raspberry sprouting between the chunks of charcoal underfoot. The brook at the foot of our hill, which dries up almost every August, is brimming with water, and this morning, I spotted a school of minnows and half a dozen husky chubs.

Perhaps, as with advancing age, the physical life becomes less important and yet, paradoxically, more precious, this green revolution against the temporary death of winter is a reminder that the earth, like our own lives, is a gift.

Thirty-five years ago this month, in a little hospital in Ohio, one of our kids was born. It was an evening like this one, quiet and green, but the Ohio spring was much farther along than this one, the oak trees in full leaf. A power mower droned on the hospital lawn, and a cardinal bright on a bush sang his optimistic, "Birdy, birdy, birdy!" In the operating room next to the delivery room where our son's life was beginning, a young Amish boy was trying not to die. He'd been careless around the farm machinery, slipped, and been drawn through a manure spreader. His anguished father, huge and full-bearded, a dark blue denim presence, sat opposite me in the waiting room, kneading his knees with hands the size of hay forks.

A doctor came into the room to talk with him. They needed blood, he said, but the Amishman couldn't understand him. A Mennonite nurse explained in German. He shook his head; he couldn't do it. The doctor turned to leave, and crooked a finger at me. A few minutes later, the nurse and I each gave a pint.

Just before midnight, while the Amishman still sat there in the starkest agony of spirit I've ever seen, another doctor came in. The obstetrician. He stuck his hand out toward me. "Well, Mr. Lange," he said, "you've got a nice healthy son!" I shook his hand numbly, my feelings scattering in all directions. My eyes could not keep away from the Amishman's. His word and mine for "son" sounded the same, and I knew he understood the doctor this time. His eyes closed, and his head shook slowly from side to side.

A few minutes later, hugging my wife and the red-faced little creature she held on her breast, I smelled the aroma of fresh-cut grass drifting in through the open window in the cool night. We were so very happy there with this new gift of life, this sturdy but tenuous thing to carry carefully with us for the next eighteen years, like a cup filled to overflowing. On my way out, I stopped and touched the Amishman's shoulder; we were related now by blood. But he was somewhere deep inside his private hell, and did not look up.

This evening, as I sit by my window looking up through green leaves, he is probably outdoors on his farm in Ohio. I suppose he leans against a fence post or a porch railing and gazes out across emerald fields, cows grazing, crows flapping toward their roosts. And I'm sure that on this vernal anniversary he remembers that long-ago night, bursting with green life and redolent of freshly cut grass, when we were both given the gift of new life. Perhaps for him—as for me just now—a robin sings in the last light of the spring evening.

Dear Olivia

ear Olivia—I hear that you and your mother came home from the hospital today, and that you're both doing just fine. We didn't expect anything different, but it's still a great relief. It was just about thirty-four years ago that your grandmother and I brought your father home from the hospital where he was born. He was a very noisy baby, and sometimes we didn't get much sleep when he was around. But he was healthy, and that was a blessing.

When your grandmother and I were young parents, as your mother and father are now, we didn't think too much about the world our children were entering. We were too busy being parents. But now that all you grandchildren are coming along, we worry and wonder a lot about what things will be like for you when you are growing up and finally going out on your own.

It'll be some years before you'll be able to read this. But, living so far apart, we probably won't get to know each other well at all. So I'll send you this for your mother to put into your baby book somewhere, and you'll come across it someday. It may mean nothing to you when you do read it. That doesn't matter; it's just the kind of thing gommy old guys do when the birth of a lovely grandchild excites their sentimental inclinations.

The week you were born was a hectic one in the world. The big news in America was that an airliner had exploded over the Atlantic Ocean near Long Island, killing 230 people on their way to Paris, and nobody really thought it was an accident. The summer Olympics were beginning in Atlanta, Georgia (I almost wrote "down in Atlanta," but for you, it'll probably always be "over in Atlanta"). And all over the globe—from Tibet to Rwanda, from Northern Ireland to Bosnia, from Chechnya to Sudan—people were beating on other people whom they thought different from themselves.

But here in northern New England the week of your birth was beautiful. We've had a wet summer, and for the first time in 128 years a July with fewer than three 90-degree days. Try to imagine that where you live! So the woods and fields are as green as we've ever seen them. The rivers and streams are full of water, and we've been canoeing as often as possible. And your grandmother's garden is blooming everywhere, almost as if it knew you had been born!

The day you were born, we had a happy coincidence. Grandmother and I went to the theater to see a performance of "Mark Twain Tonight," and in it, Mr. Twain talked about his courtship of his wife, and of how much he loved her. Her name was the same as yours—Olivia. But that very night a very sick person carried a bomb into a crowded place in Atlanta and ran away, leaving the bomb behind. When it went off, two people died and many more were hurt.

The world we are leaving you is very confusing to

us. You may not find it so, but we are older and are beginning not to comprehend a lot of it. When we were younger, we found change exciting, and took it in stride. During our lifetime we have seen the invention of television, computers, nuclear bombs, penicillin and antibiotics, satellites and space travel, and painless dentistry! But now, in the final third of our lives, we often find change threatening and ominous.

We human beings as a species understand better than ever before what will happen to us if our population continues to grow as fast as it is growing; if people continue to chop and burn down the tropical and temperate rain forests; if we continue to deplete and pollute our groundwater supplies; if the wealthy and very wealthy continue to ignore the desperate plight of tremendous numbers of their fellow human beings. Yet we are continuing to do just those things, and many others, and our generation doesn't seem to be able to grasp what must eventually happen to us. Perhaps your parents' generation will understand and try to reverse these processes, but I doubt it. Perhaps it'll be yours.

I don't really mean to sound so negative. Just remember that most older folks are sure that everything that's happened since they were twenty has been for the worse. You'll hear us saying things like, "Why hardly anybody even knows how to milk a cow anymore!" or, "These young folks with their calculators—can't any of 'em add a column of figures!" What we forget is that people will learn to do whatever they need to do, when they need it. We needn't worry.

Just as the day you were born was filled with both laughter and tears, and triumph and tragedy, the world you're coming into has the potential for both. And just as your birth is a gift to all of us in your family, each day of your life is a gift to you. You may not appreciate that till you're older; but believe me, it's true! And, strange though it may seem, the more of that gift you share with other people, the more you will have of it for yourself.

Meanwhile, I thought you'd like to know that just your being born has already been a gift to the world. I've been trying for years to get your grandmother to recycle her used office paper. No soap; she's always been too busy. But today she was thinking about what she might do to make the world a better place for her grandchildren, and guess what! She's gonna do it!

So welcome to our world, Olivia. That you may love it as we do, and find life as exciting and beautiful as we have, is the fervent hope of your devoted and distant grandfather.

The Carpenter and the Honeybee

first noticed her a few minutes after lunch on Saturday, a cold, gray, lowering afternoon full of the ominous promise of worse to come.

All morning I had been setting joists for the floor of our new house: two-by-ten planks, fourteen feet long. Not exactly exciting work, and arduous enough when working alone, but satisfying. It gives you the illusion that you are accomplishing a tremendous amount of work in a short time. During the night the planks had frozen together. Now, as the weak warmth of the November afternoon heated their surfaces, they filled the cellar below with the aroma of wet spruce.

Carrying the first plank up the ramp after lunch, I looked down and saw her for the first time. She was perched on the double box joist right at the end of the foundation, and she seemed to be trying to squeeze—impossible for her—into the tiny crack between the two planks.

Like most people, I am a mass of contradictions on the subject of nonhuman creatures. I love beef and pork, for example, but would not raise a calf or pig because I would not kill it. I can with very few pangs of conscience shoot a deer, but I try to avoid squashing spiders or snakes. I find earwigs loathsome, but centipedes humorous. Because of poems and stories read to me as a child, I have a serious Calvinistic respect for the beaver and honeybee. But I wouldn't want either of them in a car with me on the highway.

She was a honeybee. Just as I was about to put my hand down upon her accidentally, my unconscious mind hollered, "Look out!" and the reflex jerked my arm back. I staggered, out of balance. If she noticed the close call we had both had, she gave no sign, and continued to try to wedge herself into that crack. Intrigued, I put down my plank and bent down to watch her. I wondered for a moment, as I pulled my specs down my nose, the better to see her up close, how it would feel to have a bee sting right on the end of my nose.

For good and obvious reasons, most of us have never seen a bee at really close quarters. Like any perfectly designed utilitarian object, they are lovely. This one, with her big, black eyes, six sturdy legs, transparent wings, and gently tapering torso, was a little aerial tugboat whose entire life had known but one passion: absolute dedication to the community that depended upon her, and upon which she in turn was absolutely dependent. She was a food-gatherer, but in the event of a perceived threat to her community, she would instinctively defend it with a kamikaze attack whose success would kill her. Celibate, bound for life to a seven-day work week, and laced into a monosexual caste of concrete rigidity, she was what she was, a worker, and aspired—could aspire—to nothing else.

What was she doing, then, scrabbling around on a couple of half-frozen joists on a cold November afternoon? Why wasn't she home? Surely there was no pollen or nectar to gather at this time of the year, on such a day. Where was home? The nearest hives I knew of were over half a mile away, on the far side of a high ridge, and they'd probably turned in for the winter. If I'd been a good Hindu, I suppose, I'd just have passed her by. "Ah!" I'd have thought, "another creature is about to enter the transitional phase of the wheel of existence. May she be granted grace for her next incarnation!"

But Western man is an ass. Whenever another creature catches his attention, he immediately assigns it human attributes, privileges, and responsibilities. He considers it a calamity if any creature to which he has attached his affections expires or, as he says, "gets lost." He is incapable of understanding that events that he tries like murder to avoid are quite natural, acceptable, and possibly even agreeable to other species. And he has a compulsion always to be fiddling with things to try to work his will.

So right away I slipped into my first aid frame of mind: What could I do to return this poor little bee safe and happy to her sisters, who must be mad with anxiety over her absence? There was, to be honest, no doubt in my mind that a honeybee far from the hive on a November day, unable to fly or even walk straight, is a dead honeybee. But I nevertheless clung to the hope that with a little help from me she might suddenly and miraculously take wing and hum off through the woods on a beeline toward home.

Perhaps she needed a little warmth. Gingerly I

pushed the point of my pencil under her front legs. She clung to it shakily. Cupping my hands around her, I breathed warm air into the enclosure (sudden, horrible fantasy of her taking off right into my mouth!). After a minute or two, I peeked. If anything, she was in worse shape than before. Must have been the coffee I had after lunch.

Which reminded me: What do bees eat? I hadn't the faintest idea, but honey sounded right, and we had some right up in our cabin. So I set her down on the joist again, went back to the cabin, and heated up a little dab of honey on a paper plate in the microwave. I took it back, set it down, and placed her gently on the plate.

Her legs were still moving spasmodically. They carried her across the plate and right into the honey. She floundered grotesquely in it, turning onto her side. Just before she became completely mired, I fished her out again. Still staggering, she crossed my palm, leaving a little trail of warm honey, and began to try to squeeze between two of my fingers.

"I'm sorry, sweetheart, but I just don't know what to do for you," I said (hoping all the while that no friend would come upon me suddenly and ask what I was doing with a bee, a paper plate, and a dab of warm honey). Invoking the principle of the living will and bowing to the inevitable, I put her back where I had first found her, no worse, I hoped, because of me, than at our introduction.

Within an hour she had stopped moving. Before dark she had shriveled to little more than half her living size, legs folded up beneath her and her long, slender abdomen pulled into a tight curl. I remembered then her frantic groping for a hole to crawl into. So I tucked her safely down between the sill and the girder pad, where it's not likely she'll ever be disturbed, until the house is dismantled in some dim, distant day.

Requiescat in pace, sweetheart. I'd say it better if I knew the second person imperative mood. But that'll do, from one worker to another.

Pop? It's Honey

he voice on the phone was distant, unfamiliar, feminine, elderly. "Is this Ida Louise's
husband? Is she there? This is her Aunt
Loolie in California. I have a message for her about
her father, Winfield. He's in the hospital."

I felt almost as if the woman on the phone were
speaking a foreign language; the names and idioms
were at least as unfamiliar. My wife's immediate family—parents and five sisters—disintegrated violently
and bitterly a few years before we met. So I never
met her parents before we were married, and she and
I never "went to visit the folks," and I never heard the
familiar words and language that they used with each
other in better days.

It's also a bit startling—because I have never
thought of *my* wife as anything but a member of my
family—to have a cousin, sister, or aunt of hers call
her by a name unfamiliar to me and refer to me as a
sort of adjunct to a much more important associa-
tion. It occurs to me at those uncomfortable
moments that the woman our immediate family has
always referred to as "Mother" is also a daughter, sister, niece, and aunt.

It was an aunt of hers calling this time, listed
somewhere as next of kin to her father, to say that my

wife's eighty-year-old father was very ill in a central New York hospital, and that "Ida Louise," as his oldest child, was responsible for deciding the level of medical care to employ to prolong his life.

We hadn't seen the old man for twenty-eight years, and I'd met him only twice, when he'd come out of nowhere, unannounced, and shown up at our house in the Adirondacks, huge, jolly, and round as St. Nick, for a couple of weekend visits. I remember being irritated with my wife at the time for her reticence—almost like an animal fear—and her refusal to let go of our kids for him to hold. "You just don't know," was all she'd ever say about it. "You just don't know."

Then, on his second visit, his fierce and brooding St. Bernard bit our neighbor's kid; and on the way out of town, using us as a reference—just as my wife had predicted he would—he passed a couple of rubber checks that we had to make good.

There were no more visits. He called before what would have been the third, sort of testing the water. I told him that, while my wife and I were not at all eager to see him again, the Essex County Sheriff was. It was our last contact.

Over the years we heard family rumors of his wanderings—Virginia, Canada, New York State—and of his condition. He was said to be failing—a social worker reported his frequent predictions that "the girls will be coming home from school any minute now"—and on welfare. Again I was irritated with my wife. Whenever I suggested that we try to find him and see if we could help him somehow, she was adamant. I still didn't understand.

And now this phone call, to tell us that the old man finally had gone to ground in a trailer in the hamlet of Cincinnatus, New York, had suffered a stroke, and was in the Cortland Hospital. We called and got his doctor. The old man is stable, he said, but comatose and failing. Did we have an idea what his wishes for resuscitation might be? Hang on, I said. We'll be there tomorrow. We packed a few things and early the next morning, with the puppy sitting between us on the seat of the pickup, started the long drive west into central New York.

He was still a huge man. He was lying propped up on several pillows, unconscious, with an airway in his nose, breathing stertorously. I went into the room and stood at the foot of his bed. My wife, though, stood in the doorway a long time. Then she began to inch slowly into the room, as if she were afraid that, against all logic, he would suddenly open his eyes, rear frightfully up in the bed, and grab her.

But nothing like that happened, only an occasional burst of louder, almost vocal breathing. She edged over beside him, touched his shoulder, stroked his forehead. "Pop?" she said. "It's Honey. I've come to see you." She was suddenly another person. In over thirty years together, I'd never heard her speak like that—not those words, not in that tone. Surely he heard her! But nothing changed.

We called the local priest; he was there within minutes, a solid, red presence of a man for whom this situation held no surprises and only one central certainty. We spoke with the nurses and with the doctor, a bright and carefully articulate kid out of Harvard. The kidney failure was irreversible, and death imminent from uremic poisoning. He was in absolutely no pain and almost certainly would not ever awaken. Yes, a decision from us would be helpful; but first, how could they help us? We listened to their reports and decided.

We visited the funeral home. And, leaving, agreed that if people everywhere, just doing their jobs, as all these people were, could be as thoughtful and caring as these, it was hard to see how any of our problems couldn't be solved. We went out to eat, and finally, late, to our motel.

After early church Sunday morning, we went back to the hospital. We weren't expecting that there'd been any change. But there had. His breathing had become shallow, irregular, and difficult. He fought against it, and almost seemed awake. He'd been laid on his back during the night, and his covers turned down to his waist. His huge, powerful arms, virtually as thick as my legs, stuck out of his hospital gown and lay before him. I turned to see my wife staring at those arms, her eyes wide with a long-remembered, long-suppressed terror. And finally!—finally I understood what for all our years together she hadn't been quite able to explain.

She stepped to the bedside and pulled the covers up to his shoulders, hiding his hands and arms. "Pop? It's Honey," she said again in that foreign language. "I just stopped in to say goodbye. We're going down to clean out your trailer." The closed eyelids jerked open—there were no eyes inside—and shut again. He took three more small breaths, and didn't take any more. It took us almost a minute to realize that he wasn't going to. I went to tell a nurse. She nodded knowingly, went into the room, and put a stethoscope to his chest. Then she pulled the sheet up over his face, and we never saw him again.

We found the trailer and roused the landlord. While she watched us carefully, we put the few pathetic, grubby, soiled remains of an entire life into three cardboard boxes, stowed them in the back of the pickup, and began the long drive home. We'd probably be there by dark.

Is that it? I wondered. Is that the retribution for years of beating up the people who love you? Is it that simple an equation? Is it over? I looked at the silent woman beside me, holding the dog on her lap and gazing out the rain-streaked window. No, I realized, that isn't it. It continues. The most important part is what happens to the people you beat.

The Old Man at Solstice

The old man could feel it coming. More so, perhaps, because he knew they had it coming. Here it was only a couple of days before the winter solstice, and all they'd had so far had been a few little cat-cuffs: a morning of freezing rain; a night of light snowfall that left a couple of inches on the ground and nothing under the hemlocks; and only one night below ten degrees. But on a bright afternoon—a weather-breeder if ever he'd seen one, with the low sun streaming into the porch where he and his partner were working comfortably in their shirtsleeves—a puff of wind rattled the door at the south end of the porch. That was the wrong door for the wind to be rattling on a sunny day.

They quit just before dusk and picked up their tools. Then they leaned against the fenders of their pickups to talk for a few moments before heading home. The sun was gone behind King Hill. The sky where it had gone down was yellowish blue. But a few mares' tails hung immobile above Mount Ascutney to the southwest. And overhead, the contrails of invisible jet planes criss-crossed the lower stratosphere. There was moisture up there. A lot of wet weather would be coming their way in a day or two.

During the next morning the clouds began to

appear. The two carpenters ate their lunches in patchy sunshine, and by the time they'd finished them, had pulled on warmer clothes. During the afternoon, the sky thickened and darkened, the weight of clouds adding to the gloom of early dusk. They quit a little after three and dropped down off the steep hill in third gear, one behind the other, to the village below.

The old man beeped goodbye to his partner's truck and pulled in at the post office. Christmas cards, mostly, and a couple of requests for charitable donations before the end of the tax year. A yellow card; he had a package. He picked it up at the window. Something from his wife's sister; a present, he supposed. He backed out and started slowly up the street, beeping at Frank's back in the grocery store window. Frank nodded over his shoulder. Then up past the little library, remembering briefly what Andrew Carnegie had said about the shame of dying rich. Then along the brook, with ice-sheathed alder branches hanging down to the water. Past the Baptist church, candlestick lights glowing in the windows. And finally onto his own dirt road beside the swamp, with the tunnel of branches meeting overhead.

The dog was waiting at the head of the driveway, sitting right in his way with her front feet together and tail swishing the gravel behind. He knew she'd move, and kept right on going. As he turned off the engine in the garage, he saw her standing outside his door, looking up. It was obvious what she wanted. "All right, all right," he said. "Just let me get these overalls off and my lunch pail inside, and let me give

Mother her mail. I better bring a flashlight, too. You wait out here."

A few minutes later, in slowly gathering darkness, they left the yard and followed an old logging road up through sapling beeches to an ancient wall. The woods were absolutely still, in expectation of the coming snow. Far off, he could hear the rumble of traffic on the interstate. Here, except for the rapid patter of the dog's feet in the leaves, and the slow crunch of his own, he could have heard a weasel breathe.

They followed the wall, the dog sniffing the crevices for squirrels, the old man reflecting on the dull, brute strength of body and spirit it must have taken to pull those great granite teeth from the earth, drag them here, and stack them on each other.

It was the somberest day of the year. Dark: even the shortest day would be only a few seconds shorter. Cloudy: the gray-black ceiling pressing down and only minutes from snow. Cold: frozen leaves underfoot and no snowy insulation yet to soften them. Almost Christmas: the first that he and his wife would spend alone in over thirty years, with the kids far-flung to their own lives and families at the other ends of the continent. There were often tears in his wife's eyes, but he didn't know what he might do about it.

How exciting it must be, he thought, to be kids— to be on the threshold of a life! But would he like to start his again, knowing what was coming? He thought about that, weighed it in his mind, and didn't think so. On the other hand, he reflected, it had always seemed to him—and still did—that he was forever on the threshold of something new. The trick was to try to influence what that might be, and to make the best of whatever it turned out to be.

A hollow in the stone wall beckoned. He sat down against it, pulling leaves together under the seat of his wool pants. The dog, nervous about the break in routine, came pattering back and shoved her pointed muzzle under his hand. "It's all right, girl. Shh . . ." She sat down against his knee, facing away, watching the woods, on guard; that was the sheep dog in her.

He leaned his head to the right, rested his cheek against the tightly-furrowed trunk of a white ash, and listened. Not a sound but the scratch of his whiskers against his collar; yet it seemed as if something soft were already falling through the air. He and the dog sat still and watched the light fade from the woods. Trees farther off, then closer and closer, became indistinct and melted into the general dark. He thought he heard a nuthatch, softly and just once, say, "hit-hit," a few yards away.

The dog stirred; it was time to go. They turned back, with the loom of the wall to their right now. And as the lights of the house peeked through the trees, a few minutes later, he felt the first wet snowflakes against his face. Still another cycle had begun.

Well Grounded in Mechanics

he Stevenson Cemetery lies on the side of a sandy hill about two miles down the old River Road. Tourists stop in the summertime once in a while to photograph the scenery, and a couple of local schoolteachers bring their social studies classes each year to make rubbings of some of the oldest stones. The sandy soil prevents Phonse Duclos, the caretaker, from ever growing much of a lawn there. But with the big oak trees all around, the rapid river below, and the mountains rising behind it, it's one of the prettiest places in town.

Now, all the old cemeteries are repositories of hundreds of fascinating stories—most of them, sadly, forgotten. And the Stevenson Cemetery is no exception. But there's one grave there that simply begs to be explained, and, luckily, the story behind it hasn't yet disappeared. It soon will—those who know it are getting on in years—so I thought I'd write it down before they're all gone.

The grave I'm talking about is up at the top end of the cemetery, only about twenty feet from Phonse's utility shack, where he keeps his mowers and clippers and things, and where, incidentally, there is electricity. The stone of the grave itself is average-sized and ordinary-looking: the name, BROWN, in big letters at the top and only half of the bottom filled in: "Homer—Faithful Husband, 1890–1972," it says, and next to that, "Lucretia—Loving Wife, 1895–   ." Nothing unusual about any of that. Just the average, run-of-the-mill headstone of a couple of long-lived old-timers. But there's something else, if you look close, and almost nobody notices it. Probably because it looks like one of those flowerpot holders that the Catholic Daughters put on the veterans' graves. But it's not a flowerpot holder.

Its stem is a piece of electrical conduit sticking up out of the ground beside the headstone on Homer's side. Fastened to the top of this, about a foot off the ground, is a metal box, UL-approved and properly attached, designed to protect electrical connections from the weather. If you unlatch the cover, swing it open, and look inside, you will find the male end of a good-quality extension cord.

The cord runs down into the tube sticking out of the ground. On summer days, after Phonse has finished mowing around the top end of the cemetery, he runs another extension cord from his utility shack out to the cord on Homer Brown's grave, and plugs it in. He leaves it there while he mows the lower end, then rolls it up and stows it back in his shack. He closes the electrical box, tips his old blue hat, locks up, and leaves.

I knew Homer for about twenty-five years. He was one of those men who, in the days before computerized ovens and catalytic converters, could do just about anything. He was a carpenter, a plumber, an electrician, a painter—not just a good one in each case, but excellent, one of the best. He could repair any engine, shoe a horse, bake an apple pie, or mend a torn canoe. Out in the shop over his garage, he kept all his copies of *Popular Mechanics*, hundreds of them; and I never knew him to buy anything that he could make instead. Often his only blueprints were the pictures in the Sears catalog, but in his case ignorance was an advantage. His solutions to problems were often better than Sears's.

Lucretia, however, was a horse of a different color. While Homer had been born and raised in the mountains, she was an educated New York City girl. They had met, fallen in love, and married during the summer of her eighteenth year, to the everlasting distress of her family, who were summer folks. Homer was of Scots-Irish stock, she of Levantine; he was stoic and pragmatic, and she, by her own admission, "artistic"; he was shy to the point of being withdrawn, and she gregarious and sometimes just a little loud. His outdoor privy behind the shop was stocked with catalogs and his beloved *Popular Mechanics*, while her living room table displayed a neat array of *The New Yorker*, *Better Homes and Gardens*, and *The American Art Journal*. They had what is often called an "interesting" marriage. Stable enough, but "interesting."

Which would have been all right if she had only been able to leave him alone. But Homer loved nothing better than working in his shop, or guiding fishing and hunting parties, and Lucretia had no place in any of that. So just when he was his happiest, she was unhappiest. She taught art classes at the consolidated high school down at the Forks, which kept her stimulated for most of the year. But during vacations she had nothing to do but straighten up the house, read her magazines, paint a little, and look out through the kitchen window at the smug little column of smoke rising from the chimney of Homer's shop. So she used to get on him some. That's pretty much the way things stayed for years and years. Until Homer spotted the blueprints on the post office bulletin board. It was shortly after that, things got worse.

A few weeks earlier Homer had been a pallbearer at the funeral of an old friend, a fellow guide and carpenter. He'd been taken aback a bit by the ornate and expensive mahogany-and-bronze casket in which his friend had been buried. Mahogany and bronze for an old fishing guide? It just hadn't seemed fitting, somehow. That had gotten him thinking.

And then one Tuesday morning he was over at the post office waiting for the mail to be distributed to the boxes. As he idly scanned the tax notices and Wanted posters on the bulletin board, his eye fell upon a brochure that some wandering evangelist, most likely, had stuck up there. Published by an obscure organization named "The St. Francis Burial and Counseling Society, Inc.," of Washington, D.C., the brochure instructed the layman in the technique of building a simple pine box coffin. This was Homer's kind of reading. He took it down and scanned it carefully.

"Dear Friend," the brochure began, "The Society believes in simple, inexpensive, and biodegradable coffins which is the design we offer here. The assembly instructions call for simple carpentry . . . funeral costs will be minimal. Be sure your intentions are both discussed . . . as well as written out regarding using your coffin." Fascinated by the subject, Homer was hardly to be put off by the syntax or punctuation. He read on. "Use Your Coffin Now," urged the pamphlet. "Interim uses of your coffin are consistent with the goals of a personal and inexpensive funeral . . . blanket or quilt storage chest . . . coffee table . . . wine rack . . . toy chest." Homer absorbed it all. Then he came to the plans drawn by "The Society."

He was outraged. "Godfrey, look at that!" he fumed to old Franklin Wright, who was lounging against the counter next to him. "They call that a simple pine box? Judast, that ain't simple! That's junk! Why, you could do better'n that blindfolded in a high school shop class!" He stuffed the brochure into his frock pocket and took it back to his own shop with him.

"By gorry!" he chuckled to himself as he set to work, "won't Lu be tickled! Not only will she save a pile of money on my funeral, but she'll finally get that blanket chest she's been after for years." A week later he called Lucretia out to the shop to view his masterpiece. Unlike the simple knotty-pine box in the brochure, this one was of dark, clear cedar boards. It was quietly beautiful, with mitered and dovetailed joints and carved initials, and oiled and polished inside and out. Its six handles were formed from naturally curved spruce roots he'd been saving to repair guide boat ribs.

Lucretia stared at it, startled and impressed. But not, sad to say, favorably.

"Good heavens!" she exclaimed. "Where are you planning to keep that gruesome thing?"

"Why, upstairs in the back bedroom," answered Homer. "I thought it'd make"—uncertainty began to creep into his voice—"I thought it'd make a nice cedar chest for your blankets and weddin' dress and stuff . . ."

"No, sir!" vowed Lucretia. "Not on your life! That thing is *not* coming into *my* house, I can tell you that! Why, it gives me the shivers just to look at it!" And she left the shop.

Homer stood quietly for a long time, gazing at the beautiful cedar coffin. If he was the slightest bit hurt by Lucretia's rejection, his face failed to show it. He moved the box down to the garage and stored it under an old blanket on a couple of sawhorses up in front of the big Buick they almost never used. "Her house, eh?" he muttered softly to himself. "Well, I guess so. But by Godfrey, it's my garage!"

In the months that followed, Homer occasionally paused to uncover the coffin and look at it and caress its silky finish. And then one day it occurred to him that he'd never tried it on for size. So he got in and lay down, crossing his arms over his chest and closing his eyes. The first thing he noticed was that it was quite uncomfortable. The back of his head on the board bottom hurt right away, and before long his bony shoulder blades and elbows, too. So he took it back up to the shop and padded it, using some old wool batting and quilted material he'd found in Lucretia's sewing closet. He tried it out again.

This time it was quite pleasant, but it needed a pillow. So he made one, stuffing it with down from a worn-out feather tick. It was quite comfortable. So comfortable, in fact, that he kept it up in the shop and occasionally lay down in it to take a nap. Before long it had become quite a habit.

The finishing touch was the reading light. Over the years Homer had found it more congenial to read out in his shop than in the living room, where Lu was always going after him about his dirty shoes and sawdusty pants and stupid magazines. So when the village library was remodeled, and they threw away the dusty portrait of Andrew Carnegie that had hung over the mantelpiece, Homer retrieved the old brass fixture that had illuminated the painting. He rewired it and rigged it up in the coffin. And thereafter he passed many happy, oblivious hours with *Popular Mechanics*, while Lucretia inside her house, with her half-glasses perched on her nose, browsed through *The New Yorker* and sighed for what might have been.

Finally, late one winter, Homer got sick for just about the first time in his life—flu. They took him down to the Neighborhood House, but it went to pneumonia, and within a few days he was dead. When Eddie Marvin came over from the funeral parlor in the county seat to pick up the body, he was met by old Bill Broe, who'd been one of Homer's closest friends. Bill had a letter from Homer, witnessed by Teddy Morrison, the village Republican committeeman, which gave explicit instructions for the disposition of the remains, with particular attention to the coffin and its contents.

And so it was that old Homer Brown was buried in his beautiful handmade cedar coffin, with two dozen of his favorite issues of *Popular Mechanics* by his side and his brass reading light in place. So it was that the light cord was run up through a piece of electrical conduit to a box above the ground, where old Phonse Duclos, faithful to Homer's last request, can plug it in now and then. And so it is that Lucretia Brown, now in her late nineties, can never visit the grave without a shudder of disgust.

"One of these days, y'know," says Phonse, "she'll short out when I plug 'er in, and blow the fuse up t' the shack. And that'll be the end of that, I s'pose."

Willem Lange is sixty-two years old. He has most of his hair and neither of his original knees.

Will first came to New England to prep school in 1950 as an alternative to reform school in his native New York State. During most of the time since, he has been collecting stories about the unique people and places in this surprisingly funny part of the world.

During a few absences from New England in the late fifties, Will managed to earn an undergraduate degree in only nine years at the College of Wooster in Ohio. In between those widely scattered semesters, he worked variously as a ranch hand, Adirondack guide, preacher, construction laborer, bobsled run announcer, assembly line worker, cab driver, bookkeeper, and bartender. After finally graduating in 1962, he taught high school English for six years, filling in summers as an Outward Bound instructor.

From 1968 to 1972 Will directed the Dartmouth Outward Bound Center. Since 1972 he has been a building and remodeling contractor in Hanover, New Hampshire.

In 1981 he began writing a weekly column, "A Yankee Notebook," which appears in several New England newspapers. Since 1993 he has been a regular commentator on Vermont Public Radio. And his annual readings of Charles Dickens' *A Christmas Carol*, which are broadcast worldwide by WCLV Cleveland on the Worldwide Web, are now in their twenty-third year.

In 1973 Will founded the Geriatric Adventure Society, a loosely knit group of outdoor enthusiasts whose members have skied in the two-hundred-mile Alaska Marathon, climbed in the Andes and Himalayas, bushwhacked on skis through most of northern New Hampshire, and paddled rivers north of the Arctic Circle in Canada.

He and his wife, Ida, who is the proprietor of a kitchen design business, have been married for thirty-eight years. They live on a dead-end dirt road in Etna, New Hampshire, and have three children and four grandchildren.

UNIVERSITY PRESS OF NEW ENGLAND publishes books under its own imprint and is the publisher for Brandeis University Press, Dartmouth College, Middlebury College Press, University of New Hampshire, Tufts University, and Wesleyan University Press.

LIBRARY OF CONGRESS CATALOGING-IN-PUBLICATION DATA

Lange, Willem, 1935–
    Tales from the edge of the woods / by Willem Lange.
        p.   cm.
    "The pieces in this book first appeared in the Valley News,
    Lebanon, New Hampshire"—T.p. verso.
    ISBN 0–87451–859–8 (pa)
    1. Connecticut River Valley—Social life and customs—Anec-
dotes. 2. Connecticut River Valley—Biography—Anecdotes.
3. Lange, Willem, 1935–   —Anecdotes.   I. Title.
F12.C7L36   1998
974—dc21   97–35028